D0010203

Tunnels

By Virginia Loh-Hagan

21st Century
Junior Library

Published in the United States of America by
Cherry Lake Publishing
Ann Arbor, Michigan
www.cherrylakepublishing.com

Content Adviser: Dr. Todd Kelley, Associate Professor of Engineering/Technology Teacher Education, Purdue Polytechnic Institute, West Lafayette, Indiana
Reading Adviser: Marla Conn MS, Ed., Literacy specialist, Read-Ability, Inc.

Photo Credits: © Checubus/Shutterstock Images, cover; © Felix Lipov/Shutterstock Images, 4; © TTstudio/Shutterstock Images, 6; © Jaromir Chalabala/Shutterstock Images, 8; © apiguide/Shutterstock Images, 10; © Harry Beugelink/Shutterstock Images, 12; © PI/Shutterstock Images, 14; © Morten Kjerulff/iStock, 16; © Vladimir Mucibabic/Shutterstock Images, 18

Copyright © 2017 by Cherry Lake Publishing
All rights reserved. No part of this book may be reproduced or utilized in any
form or by any means without written permission from the publisher.

Library of Congress Cataloging-in-Publication Data
Names: Loh-Hagan, Virginia, author.
Title: Tunnels / by Virginia Loh-Hagan.
Description: Ann Arbor : Cherry Lake Publishing, [2017] | Series: 21st century junior library. Extraordinary engineering |
    Audience: K to grade 3. | Includes bibliographical references and index.
Identifiers: LCCN 2016032399 | ISBN 9781634721677 (hardcover) | ISBN 9781634722995 (pbk.) |
    ISBN 9781634722339 (pdf) | ISBN 9781634723657 (ebook)
Subjects: LCSH: Tunnels—Juvenile literature. | Tunnels—Design and construction—Juvenile literature.
Classification: LCC TA807 .L64 2017 | DDC 624.1/93—dc23
LC record available at https://lccn.loc.gov/2016032399

Cherry Lake Publishing would like to acknowledge the work of The Partnership for 21st Century Learning.
Please visit *www.p21.org* for more information.

Printed in the United States of America
Corporate Graphics

CONTENTS

There is a large network of train tunnels under
New York City called subways.

What Are Tunnels?

Early in history, Romans built tunnels to carry water. They built tunnels to carry away waste. Tunnels still provide these services. They're also built for **transportation**. They carry heavy things over great distances. Trains and cars increased the need for tunnels. Tunnels were also built for **mining**. Engineers study how to dig tunnels. They design bigger, better tunnels.

A tunnel opening is called a portal.

Tunnels are tubes. They're **passageways**. They're built through land. They're built underwater. They're built through mountains. Engineers study the ground. They study materials. They study how to carve out tunnels. They use tools. They study **forces**. They study how to support **load**. They make sure tunnels are stable and safe.

Think!

Think about the dangers of building tunnels. What are the dangers? How was it more dangerous in the past? How is it safer today?

Soft ground tunnels are used for subways and water.

How Do Soft Ground Tunnels Work?

Soft ground tunnels are built through soil. They're weak at the openings. Soil falls apart. This could collapse in tunnels. So, engineers use **shields**. These shields are steel tubes. They're placed at the opening. They push into soil. Forces travel from the ground. They push on the tunnels' sides. Shields stop tunnels from falling down. They hold back soil.

Tunnel linings are made of iron or concrete.

Workers clear out the area. They add a **lining**. Then, they move the shields. They work on the next section.

Like all tunnels, soft ground tunnels are **arches**. Their arches go all the way around. **Pressure** pushes on all sides of tunnels. Arches provide the best support. Load squeezes forces together. It moves down. It spreads out. Arches adjust for future load changes.

Rock tunnels, like this one in Fraser Canyon, British Columbia, Canada, are used as railways or roadways.

How Do Rock Tunnels Work?

Rock tunnels are built through rocks and mountains. Engineers make holes through sturdy rock layers. Rock tunnels don't need much support. Rocks are hard. They're thick. They stay in place. They can support themselves. But some rocks are loose. Some rocks are broken. To make tunnels stronger, engineers design extra support. They add steel ribs and **bolts**. They add steel rings and a **concrete** lining.

Engineers create many useful tools like tunnel boring machines.

Years ago, engineers blasted tunnels with **dynamite**. This was dangerous. It weakened rocks. Today, engineers use tunnel **boring** machines. The front of the machine chews up rock. It smooths tunnel walls. It keeps the surrounding rock intact. The back of the machine provides support. It bores holes in rock. It attaches bolts. It builds walls. Everything is held in place.

Look!

Find a tunnel in your town. Look at it. What type is it? How long is it? What's its purpose?

Divers help build underwater tunnels.

How Do Underwater Tunnels Work?

Underwater tunnels can be stronger than bridges. They resist tides better. They resist waves better. They resist storms better. They reach longer distances. They carry more weight. But they're hard to build. They're built at the bottom of bodies of water. Water is heavy. It pushes on all sides of a tunnel. It squeezes walls. It gushes into tunnels. It must be held back.

The Detroit-Windsor Tunnel in the Detroit River
is made of steel and concrete.

Engineers build **trenches**. They use special premade tunnel sections. They're sealed to keep out water. They're sunk into trenches and the sections are attached. Any water that leaks in is pumped out. Tunnels are covered with thick layers of rock.

Engineers also think about safety. Fires and accidents are dangerous in tunnels. Engineers build escape routes.

Ask Questions!

Learn more about tunnels. Ask a teacher or librarian for help. What are some famous tunnels? Who designed these tunnels? Who built these tunnels?

Try This!

Materials

clay, cardboard square, ruler, 10 popsicle sticks, 5 pipe cleaners that are 4 inches (10 centimeters) long, plastic spoon, water, heavy objects for weights

Procedures

1 Place clay on cardboard. Make a mountain. Make it about 5 inches (12 cm) high. Make it 6 inches (15 cm) wide.

2 Design and create a tunnel using the spoon. Have it go through the mountain. The tunnel must be 1.5 inches (3.8 cm) wide. It must be 2.5 inches (6.4 cm) high. Support the tunnel's sides. Use popsicle sticks. Use pipe cleaners.

3 Test tunnel. Pour water over mountain. This tests for cracks or openings.

4 Test tunnel again. Put heavy objects on mountain. Test the tunnel's structural strength.

Principle at Play

This activity shows the tunnel design process. Engineers think about several things. They design how to bore through mountains. They make sure there aren't any leaks. They make sure tunnels won't fall under weight. They test designs. They make changes. They test again. Use different tools. Use different materials. See what happens.

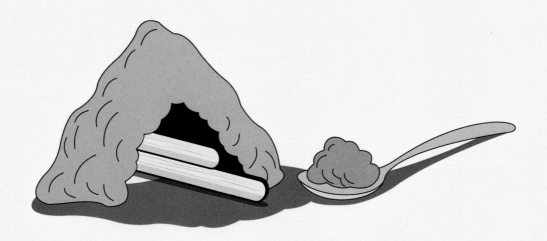

GLOSSARY

arches (AHRCH-iz) curves

bolts (BOHLTS) metal pins or bars used to secure things

boring (BOR-ing) making or enlarging a hole

concrete (KAHN-kreet) building material made from a mixture of sand, gravel, cement, and water that becomes very hard when it dries

dynamite (DYE-nuh-mite) explosive

forces (FORS-iz) pushing or pulling motions

lining (LINE-ing) covering or coating for an inside surface

load (LOHD) where weight falls in a building

mining (MINE-ing) process of extracting ore or minerals from the ground

passageways (PAS-ij-wayz) ways that allow for entering or exiting a place

pressure (PRESH-ur) force that is produced when something presses or pushes against something else

shields (SHEELDZ) devices used for tunneling to stop tunnels from caving in during building

transportation (trans-pur-TAY-shuhn) moving passengers or goods

trenches (TRENCH-iz) deep ditches

FIND OUT MORE

BOOKS

Franchino, Vicky. *How Did They Build That? Tunnel*. Ann Arbor, MI: Cherry Lake Publishing, 2010.

Latham, Donna, and Jen Vaughn (illustrator). *Bridges and Tunnels: Investigate Feats of Engineering*. White River Junction, VT: Nomad Press, 2012.

Mattern, Joanne. *Tunnels*. Vero Beach, FL: Rourke Educational Media, 2015.

Stefoff, Rebecca. *Building Tunnels*. New York: Cavendish Square Publishing, 2016.

WEB SITES

HowStuffWorks—How Tunnels Work
http://science.howstuffworks.com/engineering/structural/tunnel.htm
This site explains what tunnels are and how they work.

PBS—Building Big: Tunnels
www.pbs.org/wgbh/buildingbig/tunnel/index.html
This site describes tunnels including basics and examples.

INDEX

ABOUT THE AUTHOR

Dr. Virginia Loh-Hagan is an author, university professor, former classroom teacher, and curriculum designer. She gets scared driving through tunnels. She lives in San Diego with her very tall husband and very naughty dogs. To learn more about her, visit www.virginialoh.com.